W9-AQV-604

Date: 2/3/12

J 599.75 HAM
Hamilton, Sue L.,
Big cats /

BIG CATS

By S.L. Hamilton

VISIT US AT
WWW.ABDOPUBLISHING.COM

Published by ABDO Publishing Company, 8000 West 78th Street, Suite 310, Edina, MN 55439. Copyright ©2010 by Abdo Consulting Group, Inc. International copyrights reserved in all countries. No part of this book may be reproduced in any form without written permission from the publisher. A&D Xtreme™ is a trademark and logo of ABDO Publishing Company.

Printed in the United States of America, North Mankato, Minnesota.
102009
012010

 PRINTED ON RECYCLED PAPER

Editor: John Hamilton
Graphic Design: Sue Hamilton
Cover Design: John Hamilton
Cover Photo: Getty Images
Interior Photos: AP-pg 28; David Olson Photography-pgs 6, 7, 8, & 9; iStockphoto-pgs 2 & 3; National Geographic-22, 23, 24, 25, 26, & 27; Peter Arnold-pgs 1, 15, 16, 17, 18, 19, & 29; Visuals Unlimited-pgs 4, 5, 10, 11, 12, 13, 17, 20, 21, 30, 31, & 32.

Library of Congress Cataloging-in-Publication Data

Hamilton, Sue L., 1959-
  Big cats / S.L. Hamilton.
     p. cm. -- (Xtreme predators)
  Includes index.
  ISBN 978-1-60453-991-2
  1. Felidae--Juvenile literature. I. Title.
  QL737.C23H344 2010
  599.75'5--dc22
                    2009045260

CONTENTS

XTREME

CATS

Cougars, jaguars, leopards, tigers, and lions are just a few of the big cat predators who roam the far reaches of the earth. Strong, smart, and lethal, these cats are capable of bringing down prey much bigger than themselves.

Xtreme Fact

Big cats are silent hunters. They stalk their prey, moving noiselessly until they attack.

MOUNTAIN

X treme Quote

"Even if you've never seen a mountain lion, there is probably a chance that a mountain lion has seen you." ~Troy Swauger, CA Dept of Fish & Game

LIONS

Mountain lions are also called cougars, pumas, panthers, and catamounts. Shy and elusive, cougars live in North and South America. Lone hunters, the cats' eyes are six times as sharp as a human's. Cougars see equally well in night or day, helping them find prey that includes deer, goats, and rabbits.

Claws & Teeth

Cougars sharpen their claws on trees.

A cougar may be the smallest of the "big" cats, growing to 140-180 pounds (64-82 kg), but it is a powerful predator. A cougar uses its muscular legs to trip and jump on prey. The cat's sharp claws pin down its meal. Strong jaws and sharp canine teeth deal a swift death bite to the neck of its prey.

Xtreme Fact

A cougar can leap 30 feet (9 m) forward from a standstill.

LEOPARDS

Xtreme Fact

Yaguara is a Brazilian Guarani Indian word for jaguar, meaning: "he who kills with one leap."

& JAGUARS

Spotted big cats, such as leopards and jaguars, use their camouflage coloring to hide in trees, bushes, and grasses. Their prey often never sees them coming before the powerful predators attack.

Xtreme Quote "If called by a panther, do not answer." ~Ogden Nash, poet

Black Cats

"Black panthers" are really a dark coloring of leopards and jaguars. A rare condition known as melanism causes the cats to have black coats and skin. These cats are often found in the deep jungles of Asia and South America. It is thought that the black coloration helps them stay hidden in these areas of low sunlight.

Snow Leopards

Snow leopards are found in the mountains of central Asia. These rare cats have large paws and thick, smoky gray coats. Their coloring helps them blend in with the surrounding rocks and snow. Their snowshoe-like paws keep them from sinking in the snow. They have amazing eyesight, helping them spot wild sheep, deer, rabbits, and birds from far away.

Snow leopards have been known to kill prey up to three times their own size.

CHEETAH

SKILLS

Long, lean, and fast, Africa's cheetahs are built to catch gazelles, antelope, and even wildebeests. Cheetahs often tag team their attacks. One will begin the chase, running until tired. A second or third cheetah will pick up the race until the prey is exhausted and becomes the cats' next meal.

Xtreme Fact ▶ Cheetahs can sprint up to 70 miles per hour (113 kph) for short distances.

Fastest on Land

Cheetahs are the fastest land mammal, with bodies designed for short blasts of speed. Long tails give them balance. Their nonretractable claws perform like cleats in a runner's shoe, digging into the ground and giving them traction. Powerful legs take them from 0 to 40 miles per hour (64 kph) in 3 strides.

THE LION

& LIONESS

Lions bring strength, power, and size to the animal kingdom. Lionesses are often the hunters in a pride, but male lions sometimes add their power to hunt larger animals such as buffalo or giraffes. Reaching 10 feet (3 m) in length, and weighing from 300 to 500 pounds (136-227 kg), it is no surprise that these powerful warriors are known as the king of beasts.

Power Paws

Lions often hunt as a pride surrounding a wildebeest, zebra, or antelope. Once lions are within 100 feet (30 m) of their prey, they attack. A lion jumps on the animal's back, bringing it down. A blow from a powerful paw stuns the prey. Soon, one lion will have a suffocating hold on the prey's muzzle, and the end will be swift.

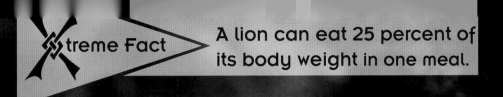

A lion can eat 25 percent of its body weight in one meal.

SIBERIAN

At 11 feet (3 m) in length and weighing up to 660 pounds (299 kg), Siberian tigers are the world's biggest cats and one of the most endangered. Only about 300 to 400 of the mighty predators live in the wilds of eastern Russia, China, and North Korea. They hunt elk and wild boar with a stalk-and-leap strategy, creeping in close, and then fatally pouncing on their prey.

TIGERS

Xtreme Fact — No two tigers have the same stripe pattern on their coats.

Tiger Tricks

Tigers have a mirror-like layer at the back of the eye called the tapetum. This reflects light and allows them to see even at night. Their 6-inch (15-cm) long whiskers are very sensitive. They pick up tiny changes in air pressure, alerting the tiger to dangers, as well as movements of their prey.

BIG CAT ATTACKS ON HUMANS

Hiker Jim Hamm rests with stitches in his head after being attacked by a mountain lion in a California state park in 2007.

Big cat attacks on humans are rare. But a hungry or threatened cat will use its claws, teeth, and muscles on what it sees as prey.

HUMAN ATTACKS ON BIG CATS

Human fear and poaching have brought many big cats near extinction. Wildlife refuges and protection laws try to help the great predators

THE

Camouflage
Coloring on clothing, skin, or fur that allows a creature to blend in with its surroundings.

Canine Teeth
The long, pointed teeth in carnivores, also sometimes called fangs.

Carnivore
An animal that eats other animals.

Melanism
A condition resulting in an unusual darkening of the fur, skin, hair, feathers, or eyes. This is caused by high levels of the dark pigment melanin. Black "panthers" are actually leopards or jaguars with melanism.

GLOSSARY

Nonretractable Claws
Claws that cannot move back into a paw.
Cheetahs have nonretractable claws. Their claws
are always out. Other big cats have retractable
claws that move in and out of their paws.

Pride
A group of lions who live together.

Suffocate
To prevent an animal from breathing.

Tapetum
A layer at the back of a cat's eyes that reflects
light. This allows the animal to see in low light. It
also causes a cat's eyes to glow in the dark.

INDEX